DISGUSTED

by Meg Gaertner

The Child's World®
childsworld.com

Published by The Child's World®
1980 Lookout Drive • Mankato, MN 56003-1705
800-599-READ • www.childsworld.com

Photographs ©: Shutterstock Images, cover, 1, 9, 10, 19; iStockphoto, 5, 6, 22 (top left), 22 (bottom left); Aaron Amat/Shutterstock Images, 13; India Picture/Shutterstock Images, 14; Thomas EyeDesign/iStockphoto, 17; Olga Enger/Shutterstock Images, 20; J. Bryson/iStockphoto, 22 (top right); Dave Pot/iStockphoto, 22 (bottom right)

Design Elements: Shutterstock Images

ISBN Hardcover: 9781503828070
ISBN Paperback: 9781622434671
LCCN: 2018944229

Printed in the United States of America
PA02395

ABOUT THE AUTHOR

Meg Gaertner is a children's book author and editor who lives in Minnesota. When not writing, she enjoys dancing and spending time outdoors.

CONTENTS

JILL'S GARDEN

Jill and her sister helped her grandmother in the garden. They planted seeds. They watered the soil. Jill had a lot of fun!

Jill's sister put something in Jill's hand.

It was a slimy worm! Jill shivered in disgust.

She did not like the garden anymore.

BEING DISGUSTED

Disgust is a strong feeling of dislike. You might feel it when you think something is gross. Not everyone is disgusted by the same things.

Some people do not like spiders. They **grimace** when they see one. Other people do not enjoy certain smells or tastes.

Disgust can stop a friend from doing some activities. But he can **overcome** his disgust.

You can get used to something that disgusts you. You can look at pictures of it. You can go look at it or smell it.

It is okay to feel disgusted. You can choose to overcome your disgust. You can also decide to avoid something that disgusts you.

THINK ABOUT IT

What tastes, smells, or sights disgust you?

Chapter Three

HELPING OTHERS

Some people might want to overcome their disgust. You can **encourage** them.

Other people might not want to overcome their disgust. You can listen to them. You can respect their feelings.

WHO IS DISGUSTED?

Can you tell who is disgusted? Turn to page 24 for the answer.